HOBBY CERAMICS

CERAMICS

Techniques and Projects for Beginners

HOBBY CERAMICS

Techniques and Projects for Beginners

Patricia A. Waller

GUILD OF MASTER CRAFTSMAN PUBLICATIONS

To Wilf, my husband, who has given me much encouragement, support and help throughout writing my first book. Also to my son Stephen and daughter Julie Anne, who both attended York College of Art and Technology, without which my path into hobby ceramics would not have begun.

First published 2003 by
Guild of Master Craftsman Publications Ltd
Castle Place, 166 High Street,
Lewes, East Sussex BN7 1XU

Text and illustrations © Patricia A. Waller 2003
© in the work GMC Publications 2003

Step-by-step photography © Mike Smith
Project photography © Anthony Bailey

ISBN 1 86108 340 8

A catalogue record for this book is available from the British Library.

Editor: David Arscott
Book and cover design: Chris Halls

Set in Goudy

Colour origination Universal Graphics in Singapore
Printed by CT Printing in Hong Kong

Preface

Until recently is has been very difficult to take up ceramics as a hobby in your own home without having to buy expensive equipment – tools, a potter's wheel and a kiln – together with a range of clay bodies, each having its own peculiarities. It was necessary, too, to have an expert knowledge of mixing and using glazes.

Today all the frustration and disappointment has been taken away, leaving the amateur to have fun with one of the most rewarding of hobbies. The sheer joy of presenting someone with a gift you have produced yourself gives both you and the recipient great pleasure. Each piece is individual, no matter how many times it may have been reproduced, and each has a professional appearance equal to any purchased from large stores.

Clay bodies differ according to the particular slip used, and for all the projects in this book I have used earthenware slip. The techniques and projects described here will provide you with a basic knowledge that will enable you to produce some stunning pieces.

Patricia A. Waller

Contents

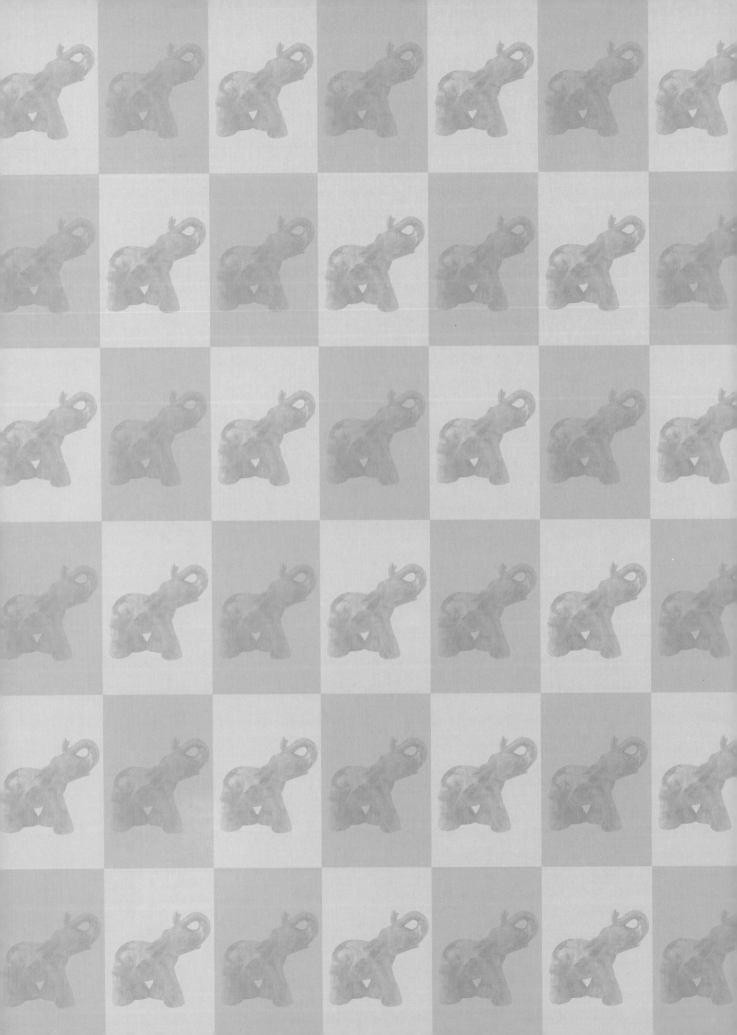

Introduction

Hobby ceramics – the art of glaze and decoration on pre-formed pieces cast from earthenware slip (liquid clay) – is a creative pastime for the enthusiastic amateur, catering for all age groups and agendas. Several stages occur before the pre-formed pieces are ready for the hobbyist to purchase. Each individual piece is first designed and sculpted from a solid block of clay. A mould-maker then makes a plaster master mould from which many plaster moulds are produced (Fig. 1), each having a limited lifetime, depending upon usage.

Fig. 1

Fig. 2

When the plaster moulds are completely dried out they are purchased by suppliers for reproduction in the form of cast ware/greenware. Liquid clay (slip) is poured into the mould, (Fig. 2), and the plaster absorbs the moisture. A variety of factors, such as temperature and the size of the piece which is being cast, dictates how long the slip stays in the mould. When the slip-caster is satisfied that the piece is ready for removal it is allowed to dry out before being put on display for purchase. The exact replica of the original sculpture from the block of clay (greenware) can now be readily reproduced in a shell-like form (Fig. 3).

There are numerous pieces available, covering a vast range of taste: functional ware for use in the kitchen, bathroom or bedroom; whimsical items such as teddies, penguins, train moneyboxes and nursery rhyme musical books; decorative pieces, including animals and figurines; mystical objects, among them fairies, dragons and wizards; Christmas trees, sleighs, snowmen, lanterns and Father Christmases; and pieces suitable for the garden, such as squirrels, tortoises, hedgehogs, figures and fountains, lights and clocks.

Each project in this book includes step-by-step instructions, together with design work or patterns for tracing where necessary, plus a list of all the materials you need. The techniques described can also be adapted to other items.

Fig. 3

Pieces can be purchased in bisque (fired) or greenware (unfired), depending on the project you are executing. If you have access to a kiln the firing range used in all projects is: bisque garden ware, mini bar 02/1120°C; greenware for underglazing, 04/1070°C; bisque non-firing (i.e. acrylics), Megga metals, etc. or glaze, 06/1011°C. Most suppliers will fire your pieces for a small fee.

Make sure when ordering greenware that you ask the supplier whether you need to take any packaging along with you. Some will pack for you, while others may expect you to do it yourself, so taking no responsibility for the pieces in transit. If the latter is the case you will need a cardboard box (the size will obviously depend on what you buy), together with material such as polyfoam chips, bubble wrap or paper shaving. Bisque will also need packing for transit, but not to the extent of greenware.

Fettling

Prior to firing, the greenware piece must be fettled to remove seam lines remaining after removal from the mould. Place the piece on a square of foam work mat approximately 12in x 12in (30mm x 30mm) and 1in (3mm) thick. It is advisable to cover the mat with paper to prevent any dust particles penetrating the foam: they can be disposed of after each project.

Before starting to fettle make sure that any barrier cream has been removed from your hands: it will make the pot greasy and the application of underglaze will therefore be difficult.

To fettle, place the greenware on the paper covering the foam work mat, holding the fettling tool at a 45 degree angle (Fig. 4). Remove all seam lines and gradually work around the piece using a very light scraping motion. Do not use the point of the tool or this will make an indentation (Fig. 5). The aim is to take the seam line level with the body of the ware.

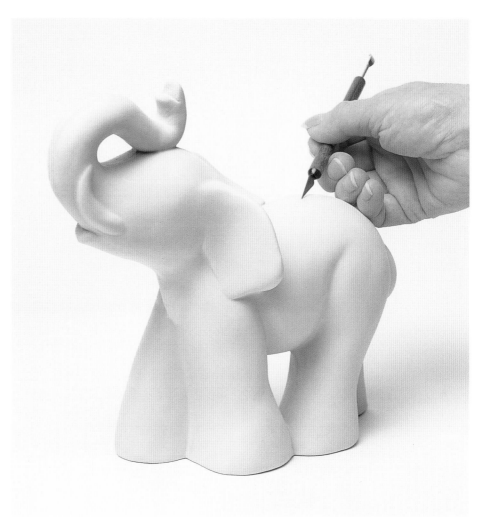

Fig. 4

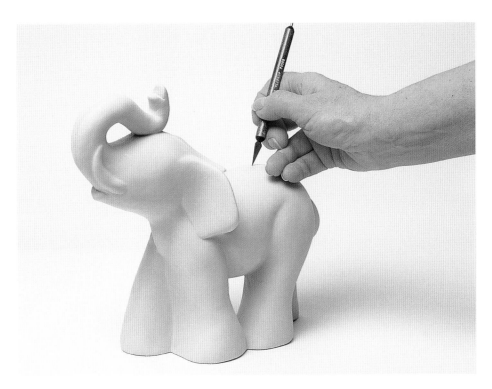

Fig. 5

Do not place any pressure on the piece, or this will inevitably cause breakage. The seam line should be barely visible at the end of this procedure: the aim is to remove the seam, not gouge it out. Dust particles should be removed with a duster brush (Fig 6).

HEALTH AND SAFETY

A disposable dust mask can be used during this stage of the preparation, since a small amount of dust particles will be produced.

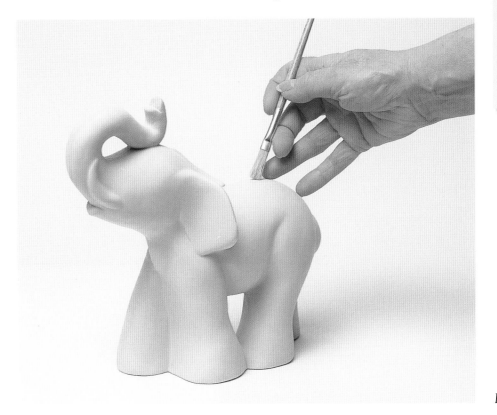

Fig. 6

Using a small piece of abrasive scrub, cover all areas in a circular motion previously worked with the fettling tool (Fig. 7).

Fig. 7

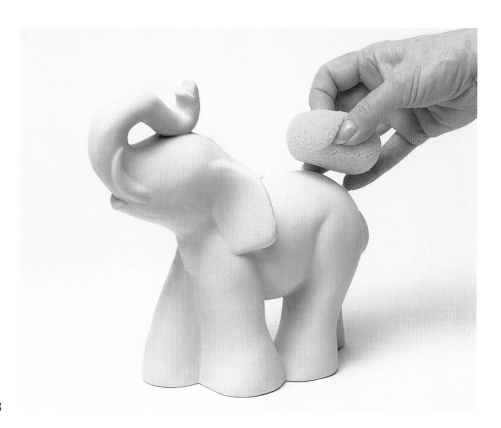

Fig. 8

Finally, using a moist (but not wet) sponge, cover the same areas again (Fig. 8). Do not touch any facial features or detailed areas during the fettling or damp sponge stage, or all detail will be lost. If this happens in other areas it is possible to scratch back lightly with the fettling tool, but do avoid facial features at all cost: a lost nose is not easily rectified.

Any slight blemishes on the ware can be rectified by dipping either the finger or a soft brush into water and then proceeding to rub carefully across the offending mark. The piece is now ready to underglaze or work on as described in the project.

Glazes

Underglaze, as the name suggests, is applied to greenware for easy coverage. The glaze contains a small amount of slip, or liquid clay, and therefore adheres more easily to the pot by soaking into the ware. Time must elapse between coats to allow each one to soak into the piece in turn. Eventually, after firing, a gloss glaze is applied all over.

Gloss glazes must be applied only to fired ware (bisque), because all the rubbish and gases which make up the clay/slip body are fired off in the first firing. Due to the nature of the glaze, such as its content, it forms a glass-like finish which in turn seals the pot. Since no gases can escape, a greenware piece will explode.

If non-fire glazes are fired in error, most of the glaze will be fired away in the kiln.

Kilns

If you progress with your hobby and decide to buy a kiln, do seek professional advice first. Most will fire up to 1300°C (2379°F), so caution must be taken. There are many small kilns on the market which can fire from a 13amp plug and are, with all the latest technology such as cut-out devices and kiln sitters, very safe. Using a kiln is not as difficult as it often first appears to the hobby ceramic enthusiast. It is fun to see a piece through the whole project from start to finish.

Taking your hobby a step further, you may eventually feel the need to buy or make your own moulds using potter's plaster then slip/liquid clay to cast. This, too, gives great satisfaction, but it can be prohibitively costly in the early stages. Do use a reputable supplier until you become familiar with each stage of your hobby.

SAFETY NOTE

Acrylics and non-firing products are used only for decorative purposes and cannot be used for functional ware. Any liquid or food will penetrate the surface, making contamination highly dangerous. Any pots or glazes that come into contact with food or liquid must adhere to health and safety regulations. Your supplier will advise.

Tools and Brushes

Always buy the best brushes you can afford at the time: cheap ones usually lose their hair or bristles in no time, making their purchase a false economy. You will come to have your own favourite brushes: those in the photograph are just a few of many.

Tools and brushes (Fig. 9)

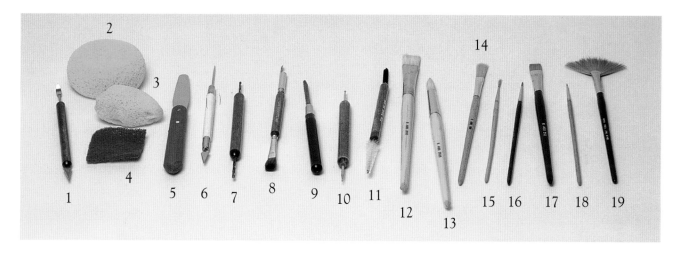

After use, all brushes must be cleaned immediately to prevent the hair or bristles from clogging and dropping out. If you have no brush-cleaner, place a small amount of washing-up liquid into the palm of your hand, gently work the brush back and forth through the solution and, when all glaze has been removed, rinse the brush in cool clear water.

Remove excess water by running the hair/bristle through your fingertips. Carefully pull the hair/bristle back into the original shape and allow to dry naturally before storing for future use, preferably in an empty receptacle with the hair/bristles uppermost. Never store the brushes wet, or leave them standing in water to clean, because the water will seep up the handle and cause the wood to split.

Non-firing glazes may be stubborn to remove, often leaving the brushes stained. However, provided that all the substance has been removed, the discoloration is immaterial. Occasionally it is advisable to give the brushes a treat with a small amount of hair conditioner, applying the same method as for the cleaning.

Tools are equally important. Make sure that they are cleaned with a scrap of waste material after use, to remove all dust particles. With care and attention they should all last many years.

1 Fettling tool.
2 Synthetic sponge.
3 Silk sponge.
4 Scrub.
5 Palette knife.
6 Lace draper.
7 Double drill.
8 Sgraffito duster.
9 Zigzag saw.
10 Stylus.
11 Double spiral.
12 Short flats bristle.
13 Pointed bristle.
14 Flat duster.
15 Liner golden synthetic.
16 Pointed golden synthetic.
17 Shader.
18 One-stroke golden
   synthetic.
19 Fan.

Projects

Pal's Shelf-sitting Ladybug and Bumblebee

Order in bisque.
Gare manufactures all glazes unless otherwise stated.

To complete, you will need the following:

Ladybug Gare mould number 3112.

Glazed white tile.

MM 6308 Deep Red.

AS 6227 It's Black.

AS 6216 Medium Flesh.

AS 6000 White.

CWS 6364 French Antique Sparkle.

Palette knife.

Stylus.

Golden synthetic pointed brushes numbers 2 and 4.

Bumblebee Gare mould number 3117.

Glazed white tile.

MM 6300 Brilliant Gold.

AS 6227 It's Black.

AS 6216 Medium Flesh.

AS 6000 White.

CPS 6128 Iridescent.

Matt acrylic spray sealant.

LADYBUG

1 AS 6216 Medium Flesh. Stir well with the palette knife. Place a small amount on a white tile. Using the no. 4 golden synthetic brush, apply two even coats to the legs, arms and entire face, including the eyes (Fig. 10). Place any remaining glaze back into the pot and clean the brush thoroughly.

NOTE

Please note: allow to dry between each stage to prevent smudging when handling.

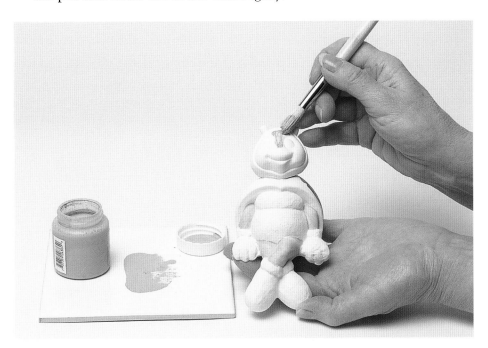

Fig. 10

2 MM 6308 Deep Red. Using the same brush as previously, apply two even coats to the wings (Fig. 11). Make sure that each coat is very smooth before applying the next. If possible, avoid the circular areas, although it is not a problem should you catch them: in stage 3 an extra coat of AS 6227 (black) will have to be applied.

Fig. 11

3 AS 6227 It's Black. Having stirred the glaze, place a small amount onto the tile. With the same brush apply two even coats to the following areas: shoes, gloves, head, both antennae and eyes. Use the no. 2 golden synthetic brush for the antennae and eyes (Fig. 12).

4 CWS 6364 French Antique Sparkle. Shake well. Because of the nature of this glaze it is best to use it straight from the pot, but the pot must be stirred occasionally to distribute the gold particles suspended in it. Using a no. 2 golden synthetic brush, apply to the stomach.

5 Allow the Ladybug to dry. Apply a dot of AS 6000 white to each eye with a stylus (Fig. 13). When totally dry, spray with matt sealant, shaking the can first.

6 Apply in short side-to-side movements, holding it approximately 10in (26cm) away from you.

NOTE

Do not spray in an enclosed area: use outdoors if at all possible.

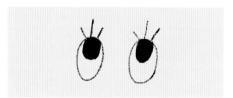

Fig. 12

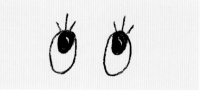

Fig. 13

BUMBLEBEE

1 AS 6216 Medium Flesh. Stir well with palette knife. Place a small amount on the white tile, using the no. 4 golden synthetic brush. Apply two even coats to the legs, arms and entire face, including the eyes. Place any remaining glaze back into the pot. Wash the brush thoroughly.

2 MM 6300 Brilliant Gold. Stir the pot well and place a small amount on the clean tile. Using the golden synthetic no. 2 brush, apply to alternate stripes on the stomach. Allow to dry. On the sting at the back of the bee continue exactly the same alternative stripes to correspond with the front. (Miss the first stripe, then follow on from there. It is advisable to place a dot of gold on each alternate stripe beforehand in order to prevent confusion.)

3 AS 6227 It's Black. Stir well. Place a small amount on the tile with a no. 4 golden synthetic brush. Apply two even coats to the following areas: shoes, gloves, head and antennae. Change to the no. 2 brush and apply two coats to the eyes (Fig. 14). Now apply the remaining alternative stripes. Make sure that all appliances, including brushes, are thoroughly cleaned before the next stage.

4 CPS 6128 Iridescent Pearl. Shake the bottle. Place some of the glaze on the tile with a no. 2 brush. Apply two coats to the inner wings on the bee's front. Each coat must be brushed smoothly and allowed to dry before the next coat is applied. Change to the no. 4 brush, repeating the technique. Apply to the wings on the back of the bee.

5 AS 6000 White. Using the stylus, place two highlights in the eyes (Fig. 15) for placement.

6 When completely dry, apply the matt sealant spray as described for the Ladybug.

NOTE

Please note: allow to dry between each stage to prevent smudging when handling.

NOTE

Please remember not to spray in an enclosed area.

Fig. 14

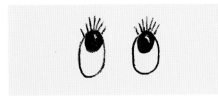

Fig. 15

Calendar Bears

> Order in bisque.
> **Gare manufactures all glazes used unless otherwise stated.**

To complete, you will need the following:

12 Calendar bears, Gare mould numbers:

January, February, March	*G2798*	*(January Champagne / February Heart / March Kite)*
April, May, June	*G2799*	*(April Umbrella / May Scholar / June Bride)*
July, August, September	*G2800*	*(July Bucket / August Melon / September Apple)*
October, November, December	*G2801*	*(October Pumpkin / November Cornucopia / December Santa)*

1 Glazed white tile.

CWS 6364 French Antique Sparkle, 3 pots.

CPS 6137 Mistletoe Kiss.

CPS 6132 Frosty Red.

CPS 6133 Misty Lilac.

CPS 6122 Oyster White.

GPS6150 Golden Peach.

GPS 6149 Golden Yellow.

AS 6000 White.

AS 6227 It's Black.

MM 6300 Brilliant Gold.

GL 4445 White Magic.

Palette knife.

Matt acrylic spray sealant.

Golden synthetic brushes nos 2 and 4.

Stylus.

1 CWS 6364 French Antique Sparkle. Using a palette knife, stir the glaze thoroughly. This glaze contains tiny particles of gold which stay at the bottom of the pot. Throughout application it is most important to stir with the palette knife, not the brush, from time to time. Because the glaze is a wash, and therefore very diluted, it is advisable to work from the pot. With a no. 4 golden synthetic brush apply two coats of glaze to the fur areas of all 12 bears (Fig. 16), but not the pads on the feet and paws.

Apply the pearl glazes to the designated areas only, making sure to wash the brush and tile thoroughly when changing colour. Shake the bottle well. Place a small amount on the white tile. Make sure to apply evenly, and brush until smooth. Using the no. 2 golden synthetic brush, apply two coats to the following areas:

PLEASE NOTE

Allow to dry between each stage to prevent smudging when handling.

Fig. 16

21

2   CPS 6132 Frosty Red. January, the dress, omitting the collar. February, the heart. July, the starfish in the bucket. August, the centre of the melon. September, the apple. October, the left-hand side only of each leaf. November, the apple. December, the hat, scarf and holly berries, omitting the fur and bell.

3   CPS 6137 Mistletoe Kiss. January, the champagne bottle only – not the labels or cork. April, the coat, omitting the collar and buttons. May, the tunic and mortar board, omitting the tassel and the raised square piping area around the tunic neck. July, the bucket, omitting the handle and contents. August, the skin around the melon. September, the tie (largest stripes only). December, the holly on Santa's hat and the parcel, omitting the ribbon.

4   GPS 6150 Golden Peach. January, the hat. April, alternate panels of the umbrella. July, the spade and sand in the bucket, but not the star fish. September, the bottom book, omitting the leaf edges. October, the pumpkin. November, the heads of the corn, but not the stalks.

5   CPS 6133 Misty Lilac. February, the bouquet. March, the triangular areas on the kite, but not the frame or tail. April, the remaining panels on the umbrella. June, the flower circlet on the head and the bouquet. September, the uppermost book, omitting the leaf edges. November, the grapes.

6   CPS 6122 Oyster White. January, both labels on the champagne bottle. March, the tails and cotton on the bobbin. May, the scroll, but not the band around it. June, the bride's gown. September, the remaining stripes on the tie. December, the fur on Santa's hat and alternate stripes on the stick in his hand.

7   GPS 6149 Golden Yellow. January, the circular blower in the bear's hand. October, the brush, but not the handle. November, the pear in the cornucopia and all the pads on the bear's feet and paws.

8   MM 6300 Brilliant Gold. Using the same technique and brush as for the pearls, apply to the following areas: January, the cork in the bottle and the diagonal stripe on the large label – covering any pearl applied previously. February, across the flowers (then rub over with a dry cloth). March, the wooden bobbin and the frame of the kite. April, the coat buttons and collar (going over any pearl accidentally applied previously), the umbrella handle and the small wooden area on the top. May, the tassel, the band around the document and the piping around the square on the tunic. June, all the flowers (then rubbing across with a dry cloth). July, the handle of the bucket.

September, the edging on each book and apple. August, the pips in the melon. October, the complete leaf (allowing the applied red to show through on one side only), the brush handle and the small circular area between the handle and the brush. November, the cornucopia basket and the stalks of the corn. December, the bell on the hat, the ribbon around the parcel and the remaining stripes on the stick. Using the wooden end of the brush, dip into the glaze and apply dots to the scarf.

9 AS 6227 It's Black to all eyes and noses (Fig. 18).

10 AS 6000 White. Using the stylus, dip into the glaze, then apply a highlight in the eye, making sure that the dot is position in the same place in each eye (Fig. 17).

Fig. 17

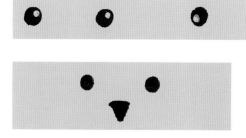

Fig. 18

11 GL 4445 White Magic. This glaze is glue-based and transparent, and may therefore be applied over other non-firing glazes to give a glitter effect when totally dry. Using the same technique and brush as previously, apply to the following areas: January, the blower, hat and labels. February, the bouquet. March, the tails and kite. April, the entire umbrella apart from the handle. May, the scroll, but not the band. June, the bouquet and circle of flowers on the head. July, the entire contents of the bucket. August, the flesh area of the melon, but not the skin. September, the tie. October, all the leaves. November, the whole sheaf of corn. December, the scarf, stick and holly.

12 When all the bears are totally dry, spray with the matt sealant. Shake the can first, and apply in short horizontal movements, holding it approximately 10in (26cm) away from each piece (Fig. 19).

Fig. 19

Cat Toilet brush holder and Kitten Toothbrush holder

Order in greenware
Gare manufactures all glazes used unless otherwise stated.

To complete, you will need the following:

Kitten toothbrush holder, mould Claymagic no. J2137.

Cat toilet brush holder, mould nos Claymagic J2130
*   & J2131.*

UG 2128 Pert pink.

UG 2105 Cocoa.

UG 2198 Pure Black.

NTG 9000 Simplicity Clear Glaze.

Fettling tool.

Scrub.

Sponge.

Duster brush.

Fan brush.

Golden synthetic no. 4.

White tile.

Stylus.

Palette knife.

Foam pad to work on, covered with paper.

1 Using the fettling tool, proceed to fettle and prepare the Greenware as instructed in the Introduction (pp. 4–7).

2 UG 2105 Cocoa. Stir well and place a small amount onto the white tile. Using the no. 4 golden synthetic brush, apply four even coats to all the stripes on the kitten and cat. Allow each coat to dry before applying the next. You will find that if you apply alternate coats to each piece they will dry more quickly. Using the same brush, apply four coats to each tail, both on the base and on the animals themselves. Apply four coats to the paws on the base.

3 UG2128 Pert Pink. Stir well and place a small amount onto the white tile. With the no. 4 brush apply four coats to the noses of each piece.

4 UG2198 Pure Black. Stir, and place a small amount on the tile. Proceed to apply four good blobs to all of the eyes in a half moon shape (Fig. 20). When dry, use the tip of the fettling tool to remove a small spot from the black of each eye and create a highlight. Using the stylus, dip into the Black and dot into the pink pads around the nose to give the appearance of whiskers (Fig. 21).

5 UG2128 Pert Pink. Shake and stir well. Place a small amount on a tile. Using the same brush as previously, apply four coats to the animals' noses.

6 Fire to mini bar 04/1070C.

7 Using the fan brush and NTG9000 Simplicity clear glaze, apply two coats to the entire pieces, including the inside.

8 Fire to mini bar 06/1011C. (Your supplier will fire for you, charging a small fee for the service.)

NOTE

Please handle with care: greenware is very brittle until fired to bisque.

PLEASE NOTE

The highlight should be removed in the same place on each eye.

CAUTION

If taking the piece to be fired, please remember to pack and handle with care.

Fig. 20

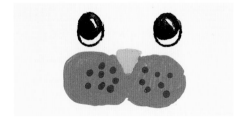

Fig. 21

Coffee/Tea Mug

Order in greenware.
Gare manufactures all glazes unless otherwise stated.

To complete, you will need the following:

Coffee/Tea Mug, Gare mould no. 2026.

(Base choice of 4): gare mould no. 2028.

UG prefix any colours you have in your own kit.

Sponge.

White tile.

Palette knife.

Scrub.

Fettling tool.

Duster brush.

NTG 9000 Simplicity Clear Glaze.

Golden synthetic brush no. 4.

Fan brush.

Foam pad to work on, covered with paper.

1 Using the fettling tool proceed to fettle and prepare greenware as instructed in the Introduction (pp. 4–7).

PLEASE NOTE

Do not hold the piece by the handle. Remember that greenware is very brittle, akin to a chocolate egg, until the piece has undergone one firing.

2 Place small amounts of different UG prefix colours of your choice on the tile with a no. 4 golden synthetic brush. Apply four even coats of the same colour to the handle and the foot of the mug. Allow each coat to dry before applying the next. Using the sponge, dip into a colour and then lightly dab onto the body of the mug (Fig. 22). Wash out the sponge for each colour. Repeat until all the colours of your choice have been applied in the same way. If you have access to a kiln, fire to mini bar 04/1070 C. If not, take for firing.

3 NTG 9000 Simplicity Clear Glaze. Pour a small amount into the mug. Hold at a 45° angle, slowly rolling the glaze around until the lip of the mug is reached. Pour off any excess glaze. Apply two coats of the same glaze, using a fan brush the entire outside of the mug. If you have access to a kiln, fire to mini bar 06 /1011°C (or get your supplier to fire it for you: a small fee will be charged for this service).

NOTE

Do not apply colours on top of each other or the effect will be lost. Any areas left without colour will fire white.

CAUTION

If taking to be fired, please remember to pack and handle with care.

Fig. 22

Heart Vase

Order in bisque.
Gare manufactures all glazes used unless otherwise stated.

To complete, you will need the following:

Heart shaped vase, Duncan mould no.3444.

Glazed white tile.

Palette knife.

Fan brush.

Sponge.

CG 7228 Emerald Forest crystal glaze.

NTG 9000 Simplicity Clear Non-toxic Gloss Glaze (¼ pint).

1 NTG 6000 Simplicity Clear Non-toxic Gloss Glaze. Pour the entire contents into a receptacle. Add a touch of cold water to make the glaze the consistency of single cream. Stir well, and then pour the entire contents into the vase. With the vase at a 45° angle, slowly turn it, allowing the glaze to roll around the inside until finally reaching the top inner ridge. Pour any excess glaze back into the pot for future use. Wipe the rim and outer edges with a sponge to remove any drips which may have found their way down the outside of the vase. Allow to dry.

2 CG-7228 Emerald Forest crystal glaze.
   Do not stir the pot of glaze. Using the palette knife, tip the top two-thirds of the glaze on to a white tile, leaving the remaining glaze in the pot. Most of the crystals will be in this glaze, making it easier to apply to the vase or any other piece at a later stage as you progress. Using the fan brush, apply two even coats of glaze to the entire outside: do not glaze the underside. Apply very carefully, not allowing any crystal glaze to drip into the inside of the vase. The crystal glaze must be butted up to the glaze on the inner rim. Allow to dry thoroughly. Place the glaze from the tile into a spare pot.

3 When dry, place the remaining crystal glaze from the pot onto the white tile. Use the fan brush with a dabbing motion (Fig. 24) rather than dragging it down the vase – this will prevent the crystals scratching any glaze applied previously. Cover the entire outside of the vase only once. When dry, fire to mini bar 06/1011°C.

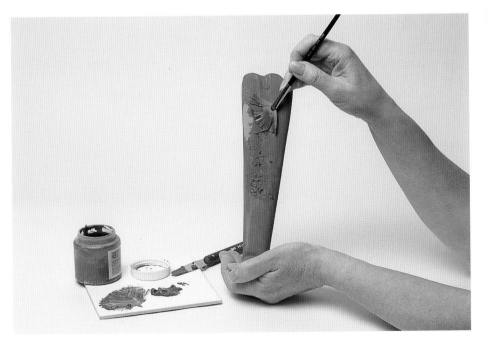

Fig. 24

Powder Bowl

Order in bisque.
Gare manufacture all glazes used unless otherwise stated.

To complete, you will need the following:

Powder bowl, Duncan mould no. DM-1431.

Glazed white tile.

Palette knife.

Fan brush.

Sponge.

NTG 9000 Simplicity Clear Glaze.

CG 7228 Emerald Forest Crystal Glaze.

1 NTG 9000 Simplicity Clear Glaze. Stir the glaze well. Using a fan brush, apply two even coats to the inside of both the lid and bowl, allowing each coat to dry between applications. Allow to dry.

2 NTG 7228 Emerald Forest. Do not stir. Tip the top two-thirds of the glaze onto the white tile, leaving the remaining glaze in the pot. Most of the crystals will be in this glaze. Using the fan brush, apply two coats to the outside of the lid and bowl (Fig 25). Do not glaze underneath the bowl. Allow each coat to dry before applying the next. Place the remaining crystal glaze into a spare pot.

3 When the piece is dry, place the crystal glaze from the pot on the white tile. Use the fan brush with a dabbing motion rather than dragging the brush across the pot (Fig 26). This method of application will prevent the crystals from scratching and removing any glaze applied previously. Apply one coat only to the lid and base. As with the previous project (see p. 31), leave a space with no crystals on the edge of the lid.

4 When the piece is completely dry, fire to mini bar 06/1011°C if you have access to a kiln, or take it to your supplier for firing.

NOTE

Crystal glazes are produced in various colours. They are all applied using the same technique. The glaze I have used is green in colour, but the choice is yours. Crystal glazes are for decorative ware only. They are not to be used on any piece which will come into contact with food.

Fig. 25

Fig. 26

Easter Duck Egg Box

Order in greenware.

Gare manufacture all glazes unless otherwise stated.

To complete, you will need the following:

Easter duck egg box, Donna mould no. D–1280.

Fettling tool.

Sponge.

Scrub.

Empty plastic container.

Piece of sponge or foam rubber (size depending on the piece being worked on).

Golden synthetic brushes nos 2 and 4.

Fan brush.

Glazed white tile.

NTG 900 Simplicity Clear Glaze.

UG 2108 Lemon Peel.

UG 2131 Golden Orange.

UG 2184 Desert Turquoise.

UG 2196 Poppy Red.

UG 2198 Pure Black.

1 Remove the head from the body of the duck container, placing both on the sponge/foam rubber. Look carefully at the pieces: you will see the seam line from the mould. Use whichever end of the fettling tool you feel happy with at a 45° angle, keeping the blade flat. (Care should be taken: the so-called blade is not exceptionally sharp, but the points are.) Do not place any pressure on the piece. Begin scraping the seam line to remove it. At this stage the whole seam will still be visible, not raised. When fettling, remember to remove the inner edge around both the head and body. The dust which has been removed should be kept to one side in a small jar or empty film case for future use should any repair holes need filling in the greenware.

   Using the small piece of scrub in a circular motion, repeat the procedure used with the fettling tool. At this stage the seam lines should be barely visible. Finally sponge the entire head and body (with a damp, rather than wet, sponge) giving the seam areas preferential treatment. At this stage it is very important not to rub excessively or all features and details will be totally lost, and this will ruin the piece. Pour a small amount of water into the body, immediately turning and tipping the liquid to the edge and then pouring off. Repeat this procedure with the head. Do not leave water standing in the pot: the greenware will disintegrate.

2 UG 2108 Lemon Peel. Shake and stir well. Place a small amount onto the glazed tile. Using the no. 4 golden synthetic brush, apply four coats to the head. Load the brush well: it is vital that the bristle

PLEASE NOTE

Take exceptional care with greenware. Remember that you are working with a shell form at the green stage (before the piece has been fired to bisque). Although not essential, it is advisable to work on a piece of sponge/ foam rubber covered with paper for extra protection when working on a hard surface, so preventing the dust from penetrating the foam.

area is completely covered in glaze. Omit the following areas: wings, feet, beak, tuft of hair, eyes, diamond design areas, semi-circular stripes and the body. With every coat butting up to the next in a vertical movement, make sure to smooth out each application. Allow drying time before the next coat is applied. When the glaze has lost the initial sheen and looks dull this is classed as dry. Throughout, keep the brush fully loaded – a dry brush will drag and remove any layers of glaze previously applied – using the same method of application to the following underglazes.

3 UG 2131 Golden Orange. Using a no. 2 golden synthetic brush, apply to the wings, feet, beak and tuft of hair. Thoroughly wash the brush and use for the following colours.

4 UG 2184 Desert Turquoise. Apply to the centre diamond and the semi-circular stripe on both the front and back of the body.

5 UG 2196 Poppy Red. Apply to the two remaining diamond designs on the front and back of the body (Fig. 27).

6 UG 2198 Pure Black. Apply to the eyes and lashes (Fig. 28). When dry refer to Fig. 29, Highlights.

7 If you have access to a kiln, fire to mini bar 04/1070°C or your supplier will fire the piece for you.

8 When fired to bisque, pour a small amount of NTG 9000 Simplicity glaze into the body, holding it at a 45° angle. Gradually rolling and tipping around the inside of the piece to the edge, pour out into the head any excess glaze. Complete the same procedure with the head. Leave both pieces upside down to allow any excess glaze to drip out. Using the fan brush, apply two even coats to the entire outside of both pieces. At this stage they should look entirely blue.

9 Repeat the firing instructions in 7, except that the firing range is mini bar 06/1011°C.

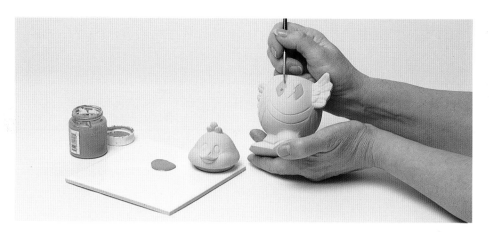

Fig. 27

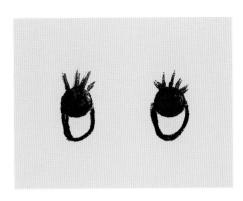

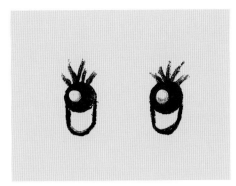

Fig. 28

Fig. 29

Fish Candle Burner

Order in bisque: ask your supplier to cut out the design areas for use as a candle burner.
Gare manufactures all glazes used unless otherwise stated.

To complete, you will need the following:

Fish candle burner mould no. Claymagic J2140.

Glazed white tile.

Palette knife.

Fan brush.

Golden synthetic brush no. 2.

Plastic film (as used to preserve sandwiches).

Plastic container or jug.

NTG 9000 Simplicity clear glaze.

NTG 9347 Bluebell.

NTG 9019 Jet-Black.

1 NTG 9000 Simplicity clear glaze. Stir well. Pour 2fl oz into the container jug. Add 1fl oz of clean water and mix well. Completely cover the exterior of the fish, not the base. Use plastic kitchen film – making sure that the film is pulled very tightly – to prevent any glaze leaking through the cut-out areas during the next stage of the procedure.

    Pour the contents of the container jug into the inner area of the fish (Fig. 30). Turn the fish clockwise slowly, tipping the glaze to the edge. Finally pour off any excess glaze. The whole inside of the fish will look blue. Allow to dry, and then remove plastic film. Using a damp sponge, remove any glaze which may have come through onto the outside of the fish.

2 NTG 9347 Bluebell. Stir well. Place a small amount on the white tile. Take the fan brush. Excluding the pupil in the eye, apply four coats to the outside of the fish. Allow each coat to dry before applying the next.

3 Apply NTG 9347 Bluebell, using the same technique as in 2 to the entire base.

4 NTG 9019 Jet-Black. Using the no. 2 golden synthetic brush, apply three coats to the pupil only. Allow to dry between coats.

5 When totally dry, fire to mini bar 06/1011°C.

PLEASE NOTE

NTG 9347 Bluebell is a garden glaze. For the fish technique it is used on normal fired wear, not high-fired as in garden ware.

NOTE

Make sure that none of the bluebell glaze passes through the cut-out holes, so contaminating the inner glaze.

Fig. 30

Tortoise

Order in bisque high-fired to mini bar 02/1120°C.
Gare manufactures all glazes used unless otherwise stated.

To complete, you will need the following:

Tortoise Gare mould no. Gare 3573.

Glazed white tile.

Palette knife.

Fan brush.

Sponge.

Golden synthetic brush no. 2.

NTG 9331 Maple Sugar.

NTG 9333 Chestnut.

NTG 9347 Bluebell.

PLEASE NOTE

High-fired bisque ware will endure outdoor conditions, but if severe conditions are forecast it is advisable to give all ware some protection. Garden glazes are non-toxic: they can be used for all other applications, including tableware.

1 NTG 9331 Maple Sugar. Stir well with palette knife. Place a small amount on the white tile. Using a fan brush, apply four coats to all areas excluding the shell and eyes (Fig. 31). Each coat must be completely dry before applying the next.

2 NTG 9333 Chestnut. Apply as in 1 to the shell only, allowing each coat to dry.

3 NTG 9347 Bluebell. Using the no. 2 golden synthetic brush, apply two coats to the eyes only.

4 Fire to mini bar 06/1011°C.

Fig. 31

Pitcher and Bowl

NOTE

This project uses the majolica technique. This involves the painting of a glaze into a gloss glaze, so that the first fuses into the second when fired.

Order in bisque.
Gare manufactures all glazes used unless otherwise stated.

To complete you will need the following:

Pitcher, Duncan mould number DM578.

Bowl, Ducan mould number DM583.

Tracing paper/transfer paper.

Pencil.

Pansy design.

Plastic receptacle.

Sponge.

Palette knife.

Glazed white tile.

Golden synthetic shader brushes nos 2 and 6.

Golden synthetic no. 10/0 liner brush.

Fan brush.

NTG 9000 Simplicity Clear Glaze (1 pint).

NTG 9404 Aqua Spice.

FS 2402 Red About It.

FS 2401 Re–Orange.

FS 2400 Butter Me Up.

FS 2405 Granny Smith.

FS 2314 Black Lab.

NOTE

When using a liner brush hold the brush in a vertical position, using the wrist movement to control the brush. It is advisable to practise first.

1 NTG 9000 Simplicity Clear Glaze. Pour the glaze into the pitcher and roll at a 45° angle, slowly tipping until the lip is reached. Pour off the excess glaze and allow to dry completely.

2 NTG 9404 Aqua Spice. Stir well to allow speckles in the glaze to distribute evenly. Place some of the glaze on the white tile. Apply two even coats to both sides of the entire bowl, plus the outside only of the pitcher, using a fan brush. Allow to dry thoroughly. Do not allow to drip inside the pitcher.

Fig. 36

3 Trace the pansy designs (Figs 35 and 36) and leaf (Fig. 37) onto the tracing/transfer paper. Using the smaller of the pansies (Fig. 36), trace at random onto the pitcher (Fig. 32). Make sure that the design fits inside the ridges.

Place the leaf design (Fig. 37) around the top edge (Fig. 33).

Fig. 32

Fig. 37

Fig. 33

4 Trace the larger of the two pansies (Fig. 35) plus the two leaves in the centre of the bowl (Fig. 34). Each petal is numbered throughout the project to prevent confusion (Fig. 35a).

Fig. 35

Fig. 34

5   FS 2402 Red About It. Place a small amount of glaze on a corner of
the white tile. If the glaze is very thick, add a spot of water until it
has the consistency of single cream. Do not over-thin or the finished
product will appear streaky. Use a no. 6 golden synthetic shader
brush for all stages of the petals on the bowl. Throughout the project,
work the bristles really well into the glaze, side-loading the brush
until it is fully loaded. Commencing on the outer edge of petal 1,
follow the shape of the petal (Fig. 38), applying two even coats of
glaze – allowing the first one to dry first. Repeat the process, using a
no. 2 golden synthetic shader brush for all stages of the petals around
the pitcher. Allow to dry completely.

6   Working within the tracing lines (Fig. 39), leave a small space
between the petals for guidance. Apply only one coat of the mixture
used in 5 for all nos 2 and 3 petals on both the pitcher and bowl. By
using only the one coat of Red About It the glaze is not so intense in
colour, and the pansy will therefore begin to have a three-
dimensional effect.

7   FS 2401 Re–Orange. Mix onto another area of the tile. Apply one
heavy coat of glaze to all no. 4 petals.

47

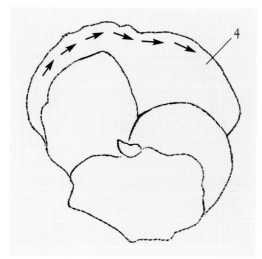

Fig. 38

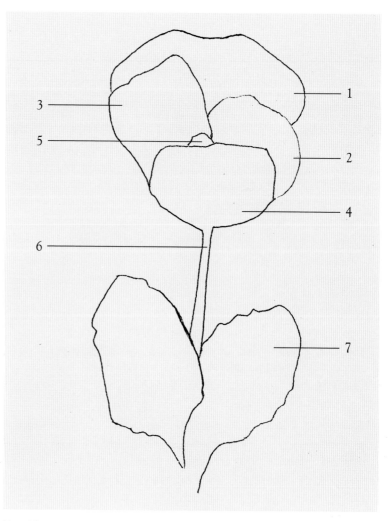

Fig. 35a

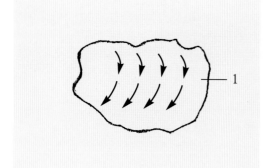

Fig. 39

8 FS 2400 Butter Me Up. Mix on the tile. Using the no. 10/0 liner brush, dab into the stamen of the pansy numbered 5.

9 FS 2405 Granny Smith. Using the no. 10/0 liner brush, apply two coats to all pansy stalks numbered 6. Then proceed with the nos 6 and 4 brushes to all leaves numbered 7.

10 FS 2314 Black Lab. Using the no. 10/0 golden synthetic liner brush, mix a small amount on the tile. (We have left all the glazes in use on the tile should any areas need touching up when the project is completed.) Outline all the pencil areas, dividing each petal around the stalks and leaves in and around the entire pitcher and bowl. Add a touch of Black Lab to Re-Orange to make it slightly darker. Do not add too much: this is only to make the piece a shade darker. Apply fine lines to the throat area of the pansy, working from the centre outwards.

11 When the piece is totally dry, fire to mini bar 06/1011°C.

Serene Elephant

PLEASE NOTE

All glazes used are gloss glazes in themselves and therefore do not need any
transparent glaze to complete the piece.

Order in bisque.
Gare manufactures all glazes unless otherwise stated.

To complete, you will need the following:

Serene elephant, Gare Mould no. 3427.
NTG 9555 Magic Flow.
NTG 9001 Arctic White 4oz
NTG 9018 Blue Lagoon.
Old towel.

Kitchen foil or clingfilm.
Palette knife.
Small container.
Liner brush.

1 NTG 9001 Arctic white 4oz. Stir well and mix in the container with half a pot (2oz) of NTG 9555 Magic Flow. Mix them together extremely well to remove any lumps which may occur in the mixture.

2 Place the towel flat onto the working area. Fold it into at least half to form a cushion (Fig. 40). Cover with one layer of either clingfilm or kitchen foil: one will work as well as the other.

Fig. 40

3 Pour the mixture from the container onto the film/foil. Spread it over the surface with a palette knife. Make sure the glaze is spread sufficiently to cover the area of the elephant.

4 NTG 9018 Blue Lagoon. Drop a small amount at random into the glaze on the film/foil. Repeat the same procedure with NTG 9008 Mauve. Using the liner brush, drag it through the coloured glazes in different directions to create a marbled effect (Fig. 41).

Fig. 41

5 Take the elephant and lay it on the glaze (Fig. 42). Roll it from side to side. Pick up the piece, turn it over and repeat the process. At this stage only the two sides of the elephant will have glaze on them. Stand the elephant upright and place to one side to allow any excess glaze to drip off the piece. You can now apply more of the glaze in 4 and repeat the procedure with a liner brush.

Fig. 42

6 Take the elephant. Place your hand underneath the towel and carefully wrap the film/foil covered in the glaze on and around the areas that are starved of the glaze. For difficult areas, such as creases on the piece, use the liner brush to dab the glaze on the elephant from the film/foil at random. Do not apply any glaze to the bottom of the feet: this piece will be 'dryfoot'. (Magic Flow will act as a host and make the glazes flow in firing.) Make sure that there is no excess glaze on the bottom edges of the elephant. Because of the Magic Flow the glazes will create teardrops if too much glaze is allowed to remain. Should this occur they can be removed with a siltstone.

7 Allow the piece to dry completely. If you have access to a kiln, fire to mini bar 06/1011°C.

NOTE

Although the piece is dry-foot, it is advisable to use a stilt-a small device which raises the piece above the batt/shelf and prevents it sticking.

Hallowe'en Pumpkin and Spooks Candle Burner

Order in bisque.
Gare manufactures all glazes used unless otherwise stated.

To complete, you will need the following:

Pumpkin and Spooks Candle Burner, Kimple mould no. 1577.
GG 1300 Fire Engine Red.
NTG 9331 Maple Sugar.
MM 6304 Copper.
MS 6037 Sterling Silver.
MM 6302 Pewter.
MM 6308 Deep Red.
MM 6300 Brilliant Gold.
AS 6000 White.
AS 6227 It's Black.
TS 6054 Walnut.

White tile.
Clingfilm/plastic film.
Small container.
Palette knife.
Sponge.
Golden synthetic brushes nos 2 and 4.
Fan brush.
Lint-free cloth.
Stylus.
Cocktail stick.
Small night-light candle.

1   Wrap the entire pumpkin in clingfilm. Pull very tightly across the eye
    and mouth areas, using GG 1300 Fire engine red. Stir with a palette
    knife, then pour into the pumpkin at a 45° angle (Fig. 43), tipping
    the piece as you roll the glaze around until the entire inside is
    covered. Tip off any excess glaze and remove the plastic film. Wipe
    any spillage off, using a damp sponge. Allow to dry.

Fig. 43

2 NTG 9331 Maple Sugar. Stir, then place a small amount on a tile, using the fan brush Apply three even coats to the outside of the pumpkin area only, omitting the following: all spooks, stalk, leaves and daggers. Fire to 06/1011°C.

3 Using the Golden synthetic brush no. 2, shake and mix the following colours and place them onto the tile: MM 6304 Copper. MS 6037 Sterling Silver. MM 6302 Pewter. MM 6308 Deep red. MM 6300 Brilliant gold.

Apply two coats to the following areas, allowing each coat to dry in between applications: Silver, to all three spooks, omitting eyes, nose and tongue. Copper, to all leaves, but not the stalk on the top of the pumpkin. Pewter, to the dagger blades only. Deep red, the spooks' noses and tongues. Brilliant Gold, dry brush across all the leaves. (Work the brush into the glaze, then proceed to remove by rubbing the brush across a piece of paper, leaving only a trace of colour in the bristles.)

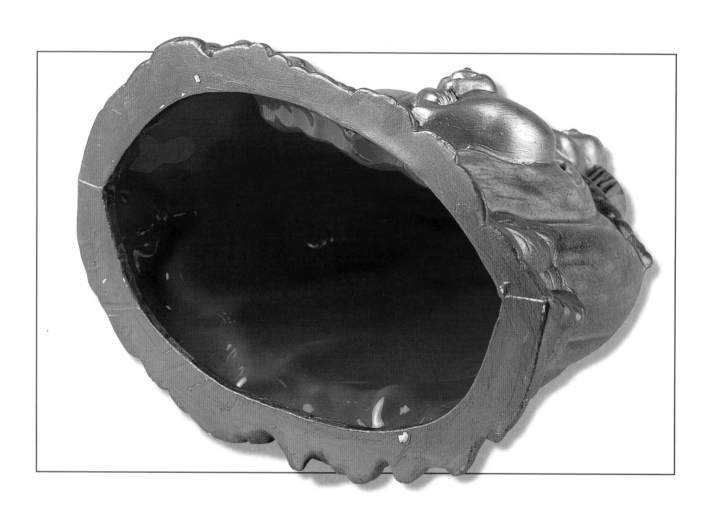

4 TS 6054 Walnut. Stir well. Apply one coat to the stalk and dagger
   handles, using a no. 2 brush. When tacky, remove with a cloth,
   leaving it mainly in the recessed areas.

5 Using the stylus, dip into AS 6227 It's Black and then apply into
   each spook's eyes. With a cocktail stick, dip into AS 6000 White and
   place a highlight in each eye. (See placement on the photograph.)

Native American couple

Order in bisque.
Gare manufactures all glazes used unless otherwise stated.

To complete you will need the following:

Native American man, Gare mould no. 2735.

Native American woman, Gare mould no. 2734.

Glazed white tile.

Palette knife.

Fan brush.

MG 7217 Bronze.

PLEASE NOTE

Metallic glazes are used entirely for decorative purposes. They must be applied to one side of the ware only: do not glaze both the inside and the outside of any project. Because of the metallic content in the glaze the pieces must never come into contact with food.

1 Working on bisque ware which has been fired to mini bar 04/1070°C, apply the glaze alternatively to both pieces. MG 7217 Bronze. Stir well with the palette knife. Place a small amount of glaze onto the white tile. Using the fan brush, apply four smooth coats to each piece, allowing to dry between each coat.

2 When completely dry, fire to mini bar 05/1046°C.

Christmas Bear with Sweetie Dish

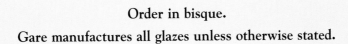

Order in bisque.

Gare manufactures all glazes unless otherwise stated.

To complete, you will need the following:

Christmas bear and Sweetie dish, Gare mould number 2812.

NTG 9000 Simplicity Clear Glaze (¼ pint).

AS 6189 It's Red.

AS 6000 White.

AS 6227 It's Black.

AS 6024 Holly Green.

MM 6300 Brilliant Gold.

CWS 6364 French Antique Sparkle.

TS 6054 Walnut.

Sponge.

White tile.

Stylus.

Palette knife.

Bristle brush, pointed, no. 3.

Golden synthetic brush no. 2.

A4 size piece of white paper.

Small piece of lint-free cloth.

1 NTG 9000 Simplicity Clear Glaze. Stir well with palette knife. Pour a small amount into the sweetie dish. Roll it around at a 45° angle. Proceed to cover the entire inside, gradually tipping to the edge, then pouring off any excess glaze. The inside of the dish should now look blue. (It will become transparent after firing: the blue colouring allows the user to see the glaze application.) Using a damp sponge, remove any drips which may have occurred when pouring off the glaze. Be very thorough, because any glaze on the outside of the dish when it has been fired will act as a barrier when applying the acrylics. Fire the dish only to mini bar 06/1011°C. The dish must be glazed in this way to be food-safe should it be used for sweets or similar.

2 Work both the Christmas bear and the dish in unison, so that one coat of glaze dries while you are working on the other piece. Stir TS 6054 Walnut. Place a small amount on the tile, using a bristle brush no. 3. Apply one coat to all areas of the bear, excluding the face, mitts, shoes and bell, and one coat to the entire dish (Fig. 44), excluding the bell. When they are tacky to the touch, rub off with a piece of lint-free cloth (Fig. 45). The raised areas will look a very pale shade of walnut, leaving the recessed areas the original walnut colour. (If the walnut has dried before you are able to wipe with the cloth, simply apply another coat and remove straight away.) This will give a three-dimensional depth to the pieces for the next technique.

Fig. 44

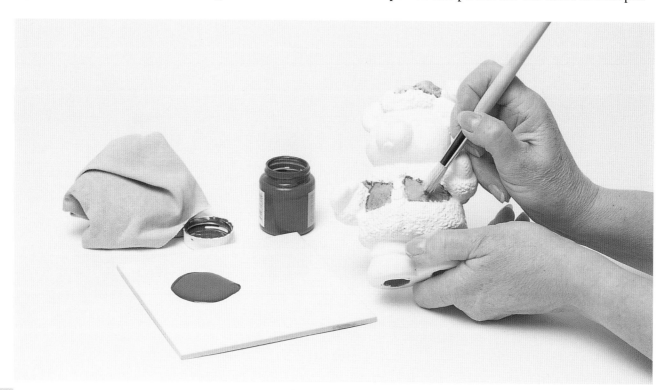

Fig. 45

3   AS 6189 It's red. Stir well, and then place a small amount on a tile. Using the same brush as in 2, work the bristles well into the red. Take the white paper and, rubbing the bristles of the brush back and forth, proceed to remove most of the glaze onto the paper. This technique is called 'dry brushing' and will give a more realistic finish to the pieces: the brush must be almost dry from the glaze.

    Working on the dish, first rub the bristles of the brush across any incised areas. They will be dry-brushed at the last moment. Keep repeating the process of loading and removing the red, gradually building up the colour on the dish until you have achieved a very soft effect. Leave the recessed areas the original walnut colour. Finally, using the same technique, give this area just one very light covering. Continue using the red with the same dry-brushing technique to the bear's coat, trousers and hat (Fig. 46).

4   It is extremely important to make sure all the red glaze is removed from the brush before proceeding onto the next stage. The bristles will no doubt be stained, but this is not a problem.

5   Using AS 6000 White and the same clean brush, apply to all the fur areas using the dry brush technique as in 3, but on a different area of the white paper. Note that the fur will not need as much dry brushing. This is important in order to achieve the effect required: the walnut undercoat must show through the fur.

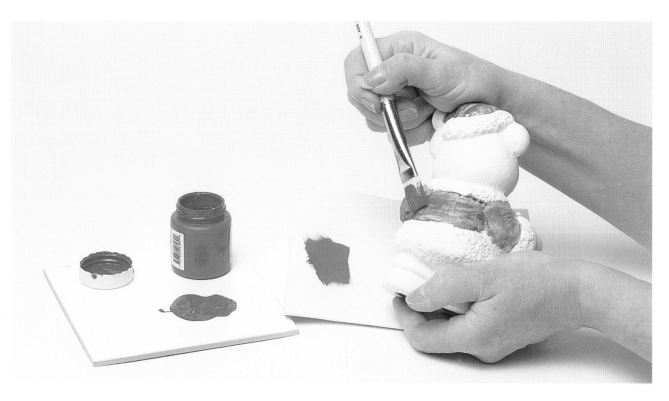

Fig. 46

6 Stir the CWS 6364 French Antique colour wash well. Because of the water consistency of the glaze, application is advised straight from the pot. It is important, however, to keep stirring from time to time in order to distribute the golden flecks evenly. Using the golden synthetic brush no. 2, apply two coats to the bear's fur covering the eyes and nose.

7 Using the same brush, apply two even coats of AS 6227 It's Black to the mitts and shoes. Make sure to stir well, and place on a tile before applying. Do not dry brush.

8 Mix the MM 6300 Brilliant Gold well, then place it on a tile. Using the same brush as in 6, apply two even coats to the bells on the dish, bear's hat and buttons. Do not dry brush.

9 Finally fill in the entire eye with AS 6000 White. Allow to dry. Using the wooden end of the paint brush, dip into the AS 6227 It's Black and place in the eye. Paint a small nose, using the same colour and brush (see photograph for all placements). Allow to dry. Using the stylus, place a tiny white highlight in the same place in each eye.

10 With AS 6024 Holly Green, dry brush very carefully across the holly leaves twice.

11 AS 6189 It's Red. Using the stylus, dot the holly berries.

12 When completely dry, spray with matt sealant.

NOTE

Do not spray in an enclosed area.

Poinsettia Dish

NOTE

Look very carefully at the design areas on the poinsettia dish, and you
will see that some of the leaves bear very fine lines. These are the petals,
whereas the broader, heavier lines are the leaves. It is advisable to scrutinise
these areas, first then mark all the petals very lightly with a pencil
(Fig. 47). This will disappear in firing. Don't forget to mark the
corresponding petals on the reverse side of the pot.

Order in bisque
Gare manufactures all glazes used unless otherwise stated.

To complete, you will need the following:

Poinsettia dish, Duncan mould no. DM 599.
White glazed tile.
Palette knife.
Sponge.
Empty jar or similar container.
Golden synthetic brush no. 4.

Fan brush.
Teaspoon.
NTG 9000 Simplicity Clear Glaze.
UG 2196 Poppy Red.
UG 2113 Holly.
UG 2131 Golden Orange.

1 UG 2196 Poppy Red. Stir the pot very well with the palette knife. Using a ratio of one part underglaze to two parts water, with the teaspoon as a guide, place three of the red to six water in the container (Fig. 48). Mix thoroughly. With a no. 4 brush apply one even coat to all the areas marked with the pencil (Fig. 49). Take care, because this is a very watery mixture and will therefore bleed into the leaves. Allow to dry.

PLEASE NOTE

NTG 6000 glaze appears blue. This is to make application easier. The glaze contains colouring to enable the user to see where it has been applied. When firing, the glaze becomes a clear gloss. Different manufacturers apply different colouring, depending upon which brand is used.

Fig. 47

Fig. 48

Fig. 49

2 UG 2113 Holly. Using the same ratio and method as in 1, apply to the remaining leaf areas, brushing into the centre and avoiding the centre stamens. Allow to dry.

3   Wipe with a damp, not wet, sponge to remove the excess surface wash on all the red petals. Continually rinse the sponge between each petal, beginning at the inner edge and working towards you. Wipe the sponge across each petal, leaving the Poppy Red in the recessed fine lines only: the remainder should have a slightly pink effect.

4   Using the same method as in 3 remove the Holly Green. You should now be left with a very pale wash effect on all areas except for the centre stamens. Continue to wipe back on the reverse side of the dish.

5   When the entire dish is completely dry, place a small amount of undiluted UG 2131 Golden Orange on a white tile. Using a stylus, dip into the colour and give a blob effect to each stamen. Apply twice more, allowing to dry each time. Make sure the pot is dry before the next stage.

6   NTG 6000 Glaze. Place on the white tile. Apply two even coats to both sides of the dish. Do not drag the brush across the dish, as this will cause the wash colours to distribute elsewhere. Apply with a very light dabbing motion.

7   When completely dry, fire to mini bar 06/1011°C.

Snowman and Snowlady

Order in bisque.
Gare manufactures all glazes used unless otherwise stated.

To complete, you will need the following:

Snowman, Gare mould no. 309.

Snowlady, Gare mould no. 308.

Two glazed white tiles.

Palette knife.

Stylus.

Sponge.

Soft piece of rag.

Bristle brush, pointed, no. 3.

Golden synthetic brush no. 2.

AS 6000 White.

AS 6227 It's Black.

TS 6054 Walnut.

TS 6051 Pine.

MM 6308 Deep Red.

MM6309 Brilliant Green.

MM 6300 Brilliant Gold.

MS 6307 Sterling Silver.

Matte sealant spray.

AS 0964 2 No-fire Snow (Duncan manufactured).

1 Robins. TS 6051 Pine. Using the no. 3 bristle brush, apply one coat, then proceed to wipe back. When the piece is tacky to the touch, rub with the piece of rag to remove excess glaze from the surface area, giving a three-dimensional effect.

2 Snowman. TS 6054 Walnut. Using the same brush as in 1, apply to the entire broom. Wipe back as in 1.

3 Snowlady. MM 6308 Deep Red. Stir well, then place a small amount on a white tile. Using the golden synthetic brush no. 2, apply two smooth coats to the snowlady's hat, but not the ribbon.

4 Snowman. Using the same glaze and brush, apply to alternative stripes on the scarf. It is advisable to mark each stripe lightly with a dot of the red beforehand in order to prevent confusion when you are applying the glaze.

5 Robins. Place a small amount of the red on the brush, and then proceed to remove by rubbing across a piece of paper. When there appears to be no glaze on the brush, rub gently across the robins' breasts. (Dry brushing.)

6 Snowman. AS 6227 It's Black. Stir well. Place a small amount on a white tile. Using the bristle brush, pointed no. 3, apply two smooth coats to the snowman's hat (but not the hat-band), the buttons on his front and his eyes. (For the eyes, follow the photograph for placement.)

7 Snowlady. Using the same colour as in 6, apply to the eyes.

SAFETY NOTE

All glazes must be used for decorative ware only.

NOTE

Allow each coat of glaze to dry before applying the next: working both pieces alternately will allow one to dry while the other is in progress.

8 Robins. Using a stylus, dip into the AS 6000 White and highlight the eyes. (Follow the photograph for placement.)

9 Snowlady. MS 6037 Sterling Silver. With golden synthetic brush no 2, apply two smooth coats to the ribbon.

10 Snowman. MS 6037 Sterling Silver. With brush no. 2, apply two smooth coats to the hat-band and the remaining stripes on the scarf.

11 Both pieces. MM 6309 Brilliant Green. Place a small amount on the white tile. Using a no. 2 brush, apply two smooth coats to the holly.

12 Both pieces. MM 6308 Deep Red. Apply as in 5 to the holly berries.

13 Both pieces. AS0964 No-fire Snow. Do not over-stir. Place a full pot on the tile. Apply with the no. 3 pointed bristle brush to the snow area on each piece by using a dabbing motion to give a snow effect (Fig. 50). It is purely a matter of preference as to how many coats of

Fig. 50

snow are applied, but I would suggest something like ¼in (6mm). Please note that as the snow dries it will settle, although more can be applied if required.

14 Both robins. MM 6300 Brilliant Gold. Dry-brush as described in 5. Apply to the entire back, wings and beak using a no. 3 bristle brush.

15 Both pieces. Dry-brush as in 14 to the holly and berries on the hats.

16 Both pieces. Place a dot of MM 6308 Deep red to a small amount of MM 6300 Brilliant Gold. Mix well – the colour should have the appearance of copper. Using the no. 2 golden synthetic brush, apply to the noses.

17 Finally, when both pieces are dry, spray with the matte sealant.

SAFETY NOTE

Do not spray in an enclosed area.

Glossary

Acrylics: non-fire colour suitable only for decorative purposes.

Batt: a kiln shelf.

Bisque ware: pieces which have had one unglazed firing, removing the moisture and debris from the clay and leaving it in a solid state.

Body: term used to describe any formula of clay.

Bone-dry: greenware which is completely dry.

Casting: filling a plaster mould with casting slip to create a clay object.

Casting slip: liquid clay for mould casting.

Ceramics: clay objects given shape when fired in a kiln.

Chamber: an oven-like receptacle with elements used to fire pottery.

Coat: one layer of glaze.

Colourwash: a self-sealing finish, decorative only, which simulates a watercolour effect on bisque.

Cone: a heat-measuring device used in a kiln.

Crystal glaze: a gloss glaze which contains lead frits and is unsuitable for tableware.

Cultured pearls: a finish, suitable only for decorative purposes, which gives a pearl-like effect.

Dry-brushing: a feathered effect brushstroke, achieved by placing colour onto the brush then removing on a piece of paper with a back-and-forth movement, leaving the brush almost dry. The colour is then built up gradually.

Dry-foot: To leave the base of a pot without any glaze when it is to be fired.

Earthenware: low-fired clay.

Fettling: removal of mould seams and any imperfections from pieces before they are fired.

Fettling tool: a tool used to prepare pieces and remove seams or imperfections in the greenware stage.

Firing: the process of maturing ceramic products by placing in a chamber and heating to various degrees.

Frit: a type of prepared glass added to certain glazes.

Fun strokes: Extremely versatile applications, having several uses. Can be watered down to simulate watercolour for design work, or used as opaque coverage by applying several coats. Used under, over or painted into a glaze as in majolica techniques. Gives good opaque coverage on bisque ware.

Garden glaze: a range of colours for outdoor use, applied to bisque. It is advisable to use on greenware, which has been high-fired. Can be applied to tableware: must have an NTG prefix.

Gem stones: A glaze which can be used on bisque or greenware. Gives a matte finish with tiny flecks of gloss body colour.

Glaze: a finish giving a glass-like surface when fired. Contains frit.

Leather hard: greenware that will hold its shape but has not reached the dry stage, retaining a dark appearance. Suitable for clay cutting.

Loading: completely filling the bristles of a brush with colour.

Matt glaze: a finish which gives sheen rather than a shine to ware when fired to maturity.

Majolica: underglaze decoration over unfired glaze.

Megga metals: non-fired metallic glazes for decorative purposes only. Not to be used for food or liquid containers.

Metallic glaze: a glaze which gives a fired, metallic effect. Pieces cannot be glazed inside when using this finish, because the piece will break in firing. Decorative ware only.

NTG: non-toxic glaze, which is suitable for use on food or liquid containers.

One-stroke: translucent glaze used for detailed work. No good for full coverage.

Opaque: a glaze which gives full coverage if applied correctly.

Pastels: Chalk to be used over a sealed surface. Each coat has to be sealed with fixative spray. Decorative ware only.

Porcelain: Clay or slip, which forms a translucent and vitreous surface when high-fired.

Pouncing: applying colour to a piece with quick up-and-down movements using a sponge or brush.

Rolling: pouring glaze around the inside of a receptacle until the whole inner area is covered. The excess is then poured out.

Sealant: usually in spray form, used over non-firing pieces to give protection. Also enhances the colours. Is not waterproof. Decorative ware only.

Seam: a ridge formed in the casting of greenware where the mould pieces are joined.

Semi-opaque: not giving full coverage.

Sgraffito: creating a design by gently scratching through applied colour to reveal the colour or clay body beneath it.

Slip: liquid clay.

Slip trailing: using slip in an applicator or applying with a brush to flow on a design, therefore leaving it raised off the piece.

Speckle glaze: a finish with a speckled appearance. Food-safe.

Stencil: paper perforated with a design to place onto a piece. Colour is then painted or sponged over it. When removed, only the design remains.

Stippling: applying colour by pouncing the tip of a brush loaded with colour against the piece.

Teardrop: A globule of glass which forms like a teardrop on the base of a pot due to excessive application of a gloss glaze when it has been fired.

Terracotta: a red-bodied clay or slip.

Transparent: a glaze or acrylic, giving translucency and enabling the under-colour to show through.

Under-glaze: a ceramic colour used under a glaze. Between three and four coats are needed to give a good coverage and prevent streaking on the finished piece. Contains slip.

Vitreous: non-porous.

List of distributors

There are so many suppliers that I have listed the e-mail addresses or websites of a selection of distributors. The remainder can be found on GARE Incorporated information@gare.com.

AUSTRALIA
Ellen Massey
mercury@ozonline.com.au

CANADA

ALBERTA
Rubyjean Ceramics Ltd
www.rubyjean.com

ONTARIO
Ceramic Arts & Craft Supply Ltd
www.ceramicarts.com

Lynwood Ceramics
lynwood.ceramics@on.aibn.com

NEW ZEALAND
Draw Art Supplies Ltd
www.draw-art.co.nz

UNITED KINGDOM & IRELAND
Cromartie Hobby Craft Ltd
www.comartie.co.uk

UNITED STATES OF AMERICA

ARIZONA
Technique Ceramics
info@techniqueceramics.com

CONNECTICUT
Satin Tone Ceramics
www.satintone.com

MICHIGAN
Tari-Tan Ceramic Supply
tmwessell@attbi.com

MISSISSIPPI
Dogwood Ceramics
www.dogwoodceramics.com

PENNSYLVANIA
A.B. Ceramics
www.abceramics.com

SOUTH CAROLINA
Ceramic Central, Inc
Lsmeltzer@homexpressway.net

TEXAS
American Ceramic Supply Company
www.AmericanCeramics.com

GEORGIA
Allison's Southside Ceramics
sall770@aol.com

KENTUCKY
Gerda's Ceramics
www.gerdasceramics.com

MAINE
Mar-Lyn Ceramics
marlynceramics@futuresouth.com

MARYLAND
Chesapeak Ceramics Supply. Inc
www.ceramicsupply.com

MASSACHUSETTS
Creative Touch Ceramic Studio
www.ctceramics.com

MISSOURI
Double Nickel Ceramics
www.doublenickel.com

NEW JERSEY
Creative Hobbies
www.creative-hobbies.com

NEW YORK
Rochester Ceramics & Greenware
john@rochesterceramics.com

NEW MEXICO
Marie's Ceramics
www.mariesceramics.com

OHIO
Adobi Ceramics
adobicer@aol.com

UTAH
Something New Ceramics
jeanut1122@aolcom

VIRGINIA
Bev's Ceramics Inc.
www.bevsceramics.com

WINSCONSIN
The Ceramic Shoppe
www.theceramicshoppe.com

WYOMING
Creations Unlimited
www.ceramicsonline.com

About the author

Formerly a restaurateur, Patricia A. Waller was inspired to switch careers after her son enrolled on a course in ceramic technology. She subsequently trained as a teacher and now gives freelance instruction, seminars and lectures on hobby ceramics as well as teaching in her own studio. Because there was no book on the subject she decided to write one.

Index

GMC Publications
BOOKS

WOODCARVING

Beginning Woodcarving	*GMC Publications*
Carving Architectural Detail in Wood: The Classical Tradition	
	Frederick Wilbur
Carving Birds & Beasts	*GMC Publications*
Carving the Human Figure: Studies in Wood and Stone	
	Dick Onians
Carving Nature: Wildlife Studies in Wood	*Frank Fox-Wilson*
Carving on Turning	*Chris Pye*
Decorative Woodcarving	*Jeremy Williams*
Elements of Woodcarving	*Chris Pye*
Essential Woodcarving Techniques	*Dick Onians*
Lettercarving in Wood: A Practical Course	*Chris Pye*
Making & Using Working Drawings for Realistic	
Model Animals	*Basil F. Fordham*
Power Tools for Woodcarving	*David Tippey*
Relief Carving in Wood: A Practical Introduction	*Chris Pye*
Understanding Woodcarving in the Round	*GMC Publications*
Useful Techniques for Woodcarvers	*GMC Publications*
Woodcarving: A Foundation Course	*Zoë Gertner*
Woodcarving for Beginners	*GMC Publications*
Woodcarving Tools, Materials & Equipment	
(New Edition in 2 vols.)	
	Chris Pye

WOODTURNING

Adventures in Woodturning	*David Springett*
Bert Marsh: Woodturner	*Bert Marsh*
Bowl Turning Techniques Masterclass	*Tony Boase*
Chris Child's Projects for Woodturners	*Chris Child*
Colouring Techniques for Woodturners	*Jan Sanders*
Contemporary Turned Wood: New Perspectives in a	
Rich Tradition	*Ray Leier, Jan Peters & Kevin Wallace*
The Craftsman Woodturner	*Peter Child*
Decorating Turned Wood: The Maker's Eye	
	Liz & Michael O'Donnell
Decorative Techniques for Woodturners	*Hilary Bowen*
Illustrated Woodturning Techniques	*John Hunnex*
Intermediate Woodturning Projects	*GMC Publications*
Keith Rowley's Woodturning Projects	*Keith Rowley*

Making Screw Threads in Wood	*Fred Holder*
Turned Boxes: 50 Designs	*Chris Stott*
Turning Green Wood	*Michael O'Donnell*
Turning Pens and Pencils	*Kip Christensen & Rex Burningham*
Useful Woodturning Projects	*GMC Publications*
Woodturning: Bowls, Platters, Hollow Forms, Vases, Vessels,	
Bottles, Flasks, Tankards, Plates	*GMC Publications*
Woodturning: A Foundation Course (New Edition)	*Keith Rowley*
Woodturning: A Fresh Approach	*Robert Chapman*
Woodturning: An Individual Approach	*Dave Regester*
Woodturning: A Source Book of Shapes	*John Hunnex*
Woodturning Jewellery	*Hilary Bowen*
Woodturning Masterclass	*Tony Boase*
Woodturning Techniques	*GMC Publications*

WOODWORKING

Advanced Scrollsaw Projects	*GMC Publications*
Beginning Picture Marquetry	*Lawrence Threadgold*
Bird Boxes and Feeders for the Garden	*Dave Mackenzie*
Celtic Carved Lovespoons: 30 Patterns	*Sharon Littley & Clive Griffin*
Celtic Woodcraft	*Glenda Bennett*
Complete Woodfinishing	*Ian Hosker*
David Charlesworth's Furniture-Making Techniques	
	David Charlesworth
David Charlesworth's Furniture-Making Techniques – Volume 2	
	David Charlesworth
The Encyclopedia of Joint Making	*Terrie Noll*
Furniture-Making Projects for the Wood Craftsman	
	GMC Publications
Furniture-Making Techniques for the Wood Craftsman	
	GMC Publications
Furniture Restoration (Practical Crafts)	*Kevin Jan Bonner*
Furniture Restoration: A Professional at Work	*John Lloyd*
Furniture Restoration and Repair for Beginners	*Kevin Jan Bonner*
Furniture Restoration Workshop	*Kevin Jan Bonner*
Green Woodwork	*Mike Abbott*
Intarsia: 30 Patterns for the Scrollsaw	*John Everett*
Kevin Ley's Furniture Projects	*Kevin Ley*
Making Chairs and Tables	*GMC Publications*
Making Chairs and Tables – Volume 2	*GMC Publications*

UPHOLSTERY

TOYMAKING

DOLLS' HOUSES AND MINIATURES

CRAFTS

GARDENING

PHOTOGRAPHY

ART TECHNIQUES

VIDEOS

MAGAZINES

WOODTURNING ✦ WOODCARVING ✦ FURNITURE & CABINETMAKING
THE ROUTER ✦ NEW WOODWORKING ✦ THE DOLLS' HOUSE MAGAZINE
OUTDOOR PHOTOGRAPHY ✦ BLACK & WHITE PHOTOGRAPHY ✦ TRAVEL PHOTOGRAPHY
MACHINE KNITTING NEWS ✦ BUSINESSMATTERS

The above represents a full list of all titles currently published or scheduled to be published.
All are available direct from the Publishers or through bookshops, newsagents and specialist retailers.
To place an order, or to obtain a complete catalogue, contact:

GMC Publications,
Castle Place, 166 High Street, Lewes, East Sussex BN7 1XU, United Kingdom
Tel: 01273 488005 Fax: 01273 478606
E-mail: pubs@thegmcgroup.com

Orders by credit card are accepted